AF270646

FOOTBALL
STRATEGIES

BY LUKE HANLON

SportsZone

An Imprint of Abdo Publishing
abdobooks.com

abdobooks.com

Published by Abdo Publishing, a division of ABDO, PO Box 398166, Minneapolis, Minnesota 55439. Copyright © 2024 by Abdo Consulting Group, Inc. International copyrights reserved in all countries. No part of this book may be reproduced in any form without written permission from the publisher. SportsZone™ is a trademark and logo of Abdo Publishing.

Printed in the United States of America, North Mankato, Minnesota.
102023
012024

Cover Photo: Bryan M. Bennett/Getty Images Sport/Getty Images
Interior Photos: Ian Johnson/Icon Sportswire/Getty Images, 5; Gregory Shamus/Getty Images Sport/Getty Images, 6–7, 22–23; Rob Carr/Getty Images Sport/Getty Images, 9; Steve Nehf/Denver Post/Getty Images, 10; Kevin Sabitus/Getty Images Sport/Getty Images, 12; John Mersits/Cal Sport Media/ZUMA Press Wire/AP Images, 14–15; Nate Fine/Getty Images Sport/Getty Images, 17; Michael Owens/Getty Images Sport/Getty Images, 19; Adam Bettcher/Getty Images Sport/Getty Images, 20; George Gojkovich/Getty Images Sport/Getty Images, 25; Focus on Sport/Getty Images, 27; Patrick Smith/Getty Images Sport/Getty Images, 30–31; Mike Ehrmann/Getty Images Sport/Getty Images, 33; Focus on Sport/Getty Images Sport/Getty Images, 34; Paul Spinelli/AP Images, 37; Rich Graessle/Icon Sportswire/Getty Images, 38–39; Doug Pensinger/Getty Images Sport/Getty Images, 41; Jason Hanna/Getty Images Sport/Getty Images, 43; Elsa/Getty Images Sport/Getty Images, 44

Editors: Charlie Beattie and Patrick Donnelly
Series Designer: Joshua Olson

Library of Congress Control Number: 2023939425

Publisher's Cataloging-in-Publication Data

Names: Hanlon, Luke, author.
Title: Football strategies / by Luke Hanlon
Description: Minneapolis, Minnesota: Abdo Publishing, 2024 | Series: Sports strategies | Includes online resources and index.
Identifiers: ISBN 9781098292447 (lib. bdg.) | ISBN 9798384910381 (ebook)
Subjects: LCSH: Sports teams--Juvenile literature. | Teamwork (Sports)--Juvenile literature. | Athletes--Training of--Juvenile literature. | Football--Juvenile literature.
Classification: DDC 796.01--dc23

TABLE OF CONTENTS

INTRODUCTION

he National Football League (NFL) has long been the most popular sports league in the United States. Its passionate fans tune in every week to witness spectacular athletic feats. Professional quarterbacks can launch the ball 60 yards or more down the field. Running backs and receivers make powerful runs or graceful catches. And on defense, strong and speedy athletes use their skills to disrupt every play.

However, behind the incredible athletes on the field is an intense strategic battle off the field. Each week, NFL coaches draw up new schemes specifically designed to beat their next opponent. Players watch hours of video to break down the opposition's weaknesses. After drilling each day on the practice field, the players put those careful plans into practice on game day. All the while, coaches watch from the sidelines and high above the field, calling plays and making in-game adjustments.

On an NFL field, the right plan can make the difference between winning and losing. Underdog teams can pull off massive upsets just by devising the right scheme during the week. And as the pressure rises in the playoffs and Super Bowl, the smallest strategic edge can mean the difference between a championship season and ending the year disappointed.

Kansas City Chiefs head coach Andy Reid talks over a play with quarterback Patrick Mahomes during a 2022 game.

CHOOSE LOVE
MAHOMES
15

Dual-Threat Quarterbacks

Early in the fourth quarter of Super Bowl LVII in February 2023, the Kansas City Chiefs lined up for a play at the Philadelphia Eagles' 5-yard line. Kansas City trailed 27–21. Both offenses had been successful all game. That was no surprise. They had been the two highest-scoring teams in the NFL during the 2022 regular season. One of the biggest reasons was the run-pass option (RPO). And the Chiefs were about to show it off once again.

Kansas City's Kadarius Toney was one of two receivers lined up on the right side

Kansas City Chiefs receiver Kadarius Toney made a big play against the Philadelphia Eagles in Super Bowl LVII.

of the field. Just before the snap, he ran in motion toward the center. Two Eagles defenders thought they recognized what was coming. They both ran with Toney while frantically signaling to teammates.

Before the Eagles could get fully set, Chiefs quarterback Patrick Mahomes took the shotgun snap. Running back Jerick McKinnon sprinted past Mahomes as if to take a handoff. At that same moment, Toney stopped in his tracks and sprinted back outside. Before the Eagles could recover, Toney had the ball on a quick pass from Mahomes. The receiver strode untouched into the end zone for the tying touchdown.

The Chiefs went on to win the game 38–35. It was a competitive and highly entertaining Super Bowl. And the run-pass option played a big part in it. The hottest strategy in modern offensive football was on full display in the season's biggest game.

RUN-PASS OPTION

The option offense has been a staple of college football since the 1940s. To mix up traditional run plays, offenses started leaving a defender unblocked on purpose. The quarterback would run toward that player's side. An additional offensive player—usually a running back—would run alongside the quarterback. This gave the quarterback two options—keep the

ball or pitch it to the other runner. Now the defender had to try to stop two players at once.

For years college teams used this running attack with great success. But while the option thrived at the college level, professional teams ignored it. With bigger and faster defensive

On the read option play, the quarterback reads the defense's reactions as he decides whether to hand off or keep the ball.

players in the NFL, there were doubts that the option could work in the pro league. Coaches also didn't want to run their quarterbacks too much because it increased the chances that quarterbacks would get hurt. However, a new style of quarterback began popping up in the league in the early 2010s. Traditionally, most NFL quarterbacks had strong arms but slow feet. They preferred to stay in the pocket and wait for a receiver to get open. The new style of quarterback was bigger, stronger, and faster. That encouraged teams to get more creative on offense.

The option had evolved by the time NFL teams began to use it. Starting in the early 2000s, college teams began running the "read option." Quarterbacks lined up in the shotgun formation next to a running back. After the snap, the quarterback would read one defender on the edge of the line and then make a decision. If the defender rushed toward the running back, the quarterback could keep the ball and run. If the defender tried to tackle the quarterback, the running back could take a handoff.

With the introduction of the read option,

ON THE RUN

A quarterback has run for more than 1,000 yards in a season only four times in NFL history. Baltimore Ravens quarterback Lamar Jackson has done so twice. Using an RPO offense, Jackson rushed for 1,206 yards in 2019. That set the record for most rushing yards in a season by a quarterback. It also earned Jackson the NFL Most Valuable Player (MVP) Award.

Jalen Hurts and the Philadelphia Eagles did a lot of damage on the ground in 2022.

rushing numbers increased for quarterbacks in the NFL. The threat of a quarterback running with the ball made an offense tougher to defend. And another wrinkle was added to make the offense even more difficult to stop. Once again taking a cue from the college game, multiple teams started to use the RPO as the core of their offenses in the mid-2010s. These are plays designed to give a quarterback three options. He can run the ball himself, hand it off to a running back, or pass. It all depends on what he thinks the defense will do. Now, instead of preparing to stop either the run or the pass, a defense has to worry about stopping both on every play.

Once a few teams had success using RPOs, most teams in the league began to base their offense around the concept. That was never clearer than in 2022. The Chiefs and the Eagles had the two best offenses in the NFL that season. And they each displayed how the RPO can help both phases of offense. The Chiefs used the RPO to bolster their passing offense. Thanks in large part to Mahomes and star tight end Travis Kelce, the Chiefs led the NFL in passing yards and touchdowns in 2022. Led by quarterback Jalen Hurts, the Eagles used the RPO to dominate on the ground. Philadelphia's offense ranked fifth in rushing yards in 2022. And the Eagles' 32 rushing touchdowns were eight more than any other team in the league.

CHAPTER 2

IN THE TRENCHES

Indianapolis Colts running back Jonathan Taylor led the NFL in rushing yards during the 2021 season. He started out the 2022 season hot as well, running for 286 yards in his first three games. However, a Week 4 game against the Tennessee Titans was proving to be a different story.

With less than nine minutes to go, Taylor had only 41 yards on 19 carries. The Titans were using a 3–4 defense, with three linemen and four linebackers. Because two of those linebackers set up at opposite ends of the line, Tennessee always had five

The Tennessee Titans kept Indianapolis Colts running back Jonathan Taylor, *right*, under wraps in 2022.

players at the line of scrimmage. That made it tough for Taylor to get outside and into open space. Once the defense had forced Taylor up the middle, he usually ran into 6-foot-4-inch, 305-pound nose tackle Jeffery Simmons. There was nowhere for Taylor to go.

However, Indianapolis still had a chance to win the game. With 8:50 left, the Colts were at Tennessee's 24-yard line. They needed one yard on third down to keep their drive alive. Taylor again tried to run up the middle. Multiple Tennessee defenders dragged him to the ground. Before Taylor was down, Titans linebacker Joe Schobert forced a fumble. The Titans recovered the ball. They had once again stopped one of the NFL's best running backs. And they had also once again proved that winning football games usually comes down to controlling the line of scrimmage.

STOPPING THE RUN

The NFL played its first season in 1920. In those early days, offenses relied heavily on running plays. Defenses responded by crowding the line of scrimmage to stop the run. Passing eventually worked its way into the league as offenses evolved. Once passing became a bigger part of the game, defenses needed to adapt while still being able to slow opposing rushing attacks.

In the NFL's early days, running was a much bigger part of the offensive game than passing.

In 1950 the Cleveland Browns were scoring at will against almost every team they faced. The one exception was the New York Giants. New York head coach Steve Owen started using a 6–1–4 defense. The Giants put six players on the line of scrimmage, but the two on the end could drift off the line to help defend the pass. It was an early version of the 4–3 defense, which uses four defensive linemen and three linebackers. With this defense, the Giants held the Browns to 21 total points in three meetings that season. By 1956 New York was using the 4–3 formation regularly. Their tough defense helped the Giants win that year's NFL title. Soon other teams copied New York's plan.

While the original concept of the 4–3 was created to stop the pass, it's also highly effective against the run. Using four defensive linemen helps occupy the offensive linemen. That gives the three linebackers a chance to fill any gaps the offense might try to run through. The 4–3 is still in use today around the NFL. In the 2022 season, the San Francisco 49ers used a 4–3 and allowed the fewest points in the league. Their ability to stop the run was a big factor. San Francisco had a lot of depth on the defensive line. Star middle linebacker Fred Warner filled gaps with ease. The 49ers allowed the second-fewest rushing yards in the NFL in 2022.

SHIFTING THE LINE

Teams that don't use the 4–3 usually play a 3–4 defense. While both formations aim to do the same thing, they get there in different ways. The 3–4 uses three defensive linemen and four linebackers. The two outside linebackers often start on

Fred Warner led a stingy San Francisco 49ers defense in 2022.

the edges of the line. Linebackers are generally smaller and faster than hulking linemen. Having more linebackers on the field gives defenses more speed and versatility to deal with faster offenses.

Jeffery Simmons of the Tennessee Titans is one of the game's toughest nose tackles.

The 3–4 was originally created in the 1940s at the University of Oklahoma. It didn't become popular at the pro level until the early 1970s. But in 1972 the Miami Dolphins used a 3–4. They became the first NFL team to finish a season undefeated and win the Super Bowl. Other teams took notice. Just as with the 4–3 in the 1960s, the 3–4 was used throughout the league in the 1970s and 1980s.

The key to stopping the run in a 3–4 is having a dominant nose tackle in the middle of the line. The nose tackle's job is to occupy as many offensive linemen as possible so the inside linebackers can fill gaps and the outside linebackers can seal the edges of the line. Tennessee's Simmons is a perfect example. With his size and strength, two offensive linemen are usually needed to block him. If they don't double-team him, Simmons can beat one blocker and get into the backfield in a hurry. With Simmons in the middle of the line, the Titans allowed the fewest rushing yards in the NFL during the 2022 season.

CHAPTER 3

Airing It Out

The Los Angeles Rams hadn't been able to run the ball all game in Super Bowl LVI in February 2022. Anytime they tried, the Cincinnati Bengals' defense stopped them in a hurry. When the Rams got the ball late in the fourth quarter, they decided they would need to win the game through the air.

With less than five minutes to play, the Rams were at their own 37-yard line, trailing 20–16. Three short passes got the Rams past midfield. Quarterback Matthew Stafford then zeroed in on wide receiver Cooper Kupp, who led the NFL in receptions,

Los Angeles Rams receiver Cooper Kupp (10) made the Cincinnati Bengals pay in Super Bowl LVI.

receiving yards, and receiving touchdowns during the 2021 season. Stafford hit Kupp for a 22-yard gain over the middle of the field. Another completion to Kupp put the Rams inside the red zone.

Stafford went back to Kupp two more times. Both plays drew defensive holding penalties. That put the ball at the 1-yard line. After another failed run, the Rams knew what to do. With 1:29 remaining, Kupp lined up to the right of Stafford. Once the play started, Stafford hoisted the ball high toward Kupp, who was covered by one defensive back. Kupp spotted the ball and brought it in for a touchdown. Relying on the passing game helped the Rams beat the Bengals 23–20 to become Super Bowl champions.

CHANGING THE GAME

The NFL changed its passing rules in 1933. Before then, quarterbacks had to be at least five yards behind the line of scrimmage when they passed the ball. That five-yard rule was eliminated. But throwing the ball was still a challenge. Defensive backs could bump receivers anywhere on the field. Getting open for passes was difficult. In the 1970s, the NFL wanted to increase scoring, so the league made more rule changes. Now defensive backs could bump receivers only within five yards of the line of scrimmage. Receivers could get

Physical cornerbacks such as Mel Blount of the Pittsburgh Steelers made life difficult for wide receivers.

open more easily. Passing offenses quickly took advantage of all the space they had to work with.

Two coaches soon devised offenses that used the pass to open up the field. One of them was Bill Walsh. While he was an

Mel Blount Rule

Mel Blount was a Hall of Fame cornerback for the Pittsburgh Steelers from 1970 to 1983. Blount was so well known for his physical play against opposing wide receivers that the new rule the NFL instituted in 1978 regarding downfield contact became known as the "Mel Blount Rule." With receivers more free to operate downfield, offenses included more passing in their game plans. But Blount remained one of the top cornerbacks in the game. He played six more seasons after the rule change, making 22 interceptions and three Pro Bowl appearances.

assistant coach for the Bengals during the early 1970s, Walsh came up with the design of the West Coast offense. It used short, horizontal passing routes to create open targets for quarterbacks. Walsh went on to coach the San Francisco 49ers to three Super Bowl championships. His short passing game was perfected by Hall of Fame quarterback Joe Montana and Hall of Fame wide receiver Jerry Rice, who shattered NFL records in Walsh's offense.

In the late 1970s, Don Coryell was the head coach of the San Diego Chargers. He came up with a pass-heavy offensive scheme. But the "Air Coryell" offense relied more on deep passing plays to stretch the defense.

Coryell focused on creating mismatches with his offensive talent. After the rule change preventing defensive backs

Bill Walsh, shown with quarterback Joe Montana, was an offensive innovator and a three-time Super Bowl champion with the San Francisco 49ers.

from making contact more than five yards past the line of scrimmage, defending deep passes became more difficult. Coryell often ran wide receivers deep down the field to exploit that. For shorter passes in his offense, Coryell relied on one running back and two tight ends. In his eight full seasons in San Diego, Coryell's Chargers led the league in passing yards seven times.

PASSING BOOM

The DNA of both these systems still remains in NFL offenses. The New England Patriots used an Air Coryell–style offense in the 2007 season. Quarterback Tom Brady's strong arm and the speed of Hall of Fame wide receiver Randy Moss proved to be lethal. The Patriots finished the regular season 16–0 and scored the most points in NFL history at the time.

That Patriots team was also the first in NFL history to run the majority of its offensive snaps in the shotgun formation. The shotgun provides more time for the quarterback to find

NFL's Top 10 Passing Seasons of All Time

Rank	Player	Yards	Year/Team
1	Peyton Manning	5,477	2013 Denver Broncos
2	Drew Brees	5,476	2011 New Orleans Saints
3	Tom Brady	5,316	2021 Tampa Bay Buccaneers
4	Patrick Mahomes	5,250	2022 Kansas City Chiefs
5	Tom Brady	5,235	2011 New England Patriots
6	Drew Brees	5,208	2016 New Orleans Saints
7	Drew Brees	5,177	2012 New Orleans Saints
8	Drew Brees	5,162	2013 New Orleans Saints
9	Ben Roethlisberger	5,129	2018 Pittsburgh Steelers
10	Jameis Winston	5,109	2019 Tampa Bay Buccaneers

a receiver. Soon more teams started to do the same. By 2013 more than half of the plays run in the entire league were out of the shotgun. In 2021 the Baltimore Ravens and Arizona Cardinals ran more than 90 percent of their plays out of the shotgun.

In the West Coast offense, the quarterback usually takes the snap under center. But even though teams use the shotgun routinely now, it doesn't mean they don't use concepts from the West Coast offense. Many coaches in the NFL today worked for Walsh or studied his system. One of them is Kansas City Chiefs head coach Andy Reid. His effective passing offense is heavily based on Walsh's creation.

Many teams follow the West Coast philosophy of using short passes instead of runs to move the ball. The norm in the NFL for decades was to run the ball on first down. It was seen as a safer way to gain yards. Walsh liked to pass on first down. A lot of teams in today's NFL do as well. In 2021, 14 teams passed the ball on at least half of their first-down plays. The added popularity of the shotgun and first-down passes helped explain why passing numbers continued to climb throughout the 2010s and 2020s.

CHAPTER 4

NOTHING DEEP

Midway through the third quarter of Super Bowl LV in February 2021, the Tampa Bay Buccaneers had held the Kansas City Chiefs' high-powered offense to just three field goals. The Tampa Bay defense had done it by tormenting Kansas City's star quarterback, Patrick Mahomes, all game. Leading 28–9 with time running short, Tampa Bay knew the Chiefs would have to pass their way back into the game. The Buccaneers knew just what to do.

Kansas City was on its own 28-yard line. On second-and-seven, Mahomes

Shaquil Barrett of the Tampa Bay Buccaneers closes in on Patrick Mahomes during Super Bowl LV.

BARRETT
58
HOMES
5

dropped back to pass. As he scanned the field, he saw no open receivers. The Buccaneers had seven players back in coverage. Two safeties played deep down the middle to take away any long pass attempt. This is known as a Cover 2 defense. The pocket collapsed. Tampa Bay linebacker Shaquil Barrett quickly wrapped up Mahomes for a sack. Even with only four players rushing the passer, the Buccaneers were able to get the takedown.

On the next play, Tampa Bay blitzed, and the pressure forced Mahomes to hurry on a deep throw. The ball was tipped by cornerback Mike Edwards and then intercepted by safety Antoine Winfield Jr. That was one of only five times the Buccaneers had blitzed in the entire game. Because the Chiefs had speedy wide receiver Tyreek Hill in the lineup, the Bucs wanted as many players as possible covering the deep part of the field.

The game plan worked, and Tampa Bay won 31–9. Mahomes was held without a touchdown pass for the first time in 31 games. That's because the Buccaneers' defense put on a master class on how to run a Cover 2.

STOPPING THE PASS

As passing offenses became more popular and more complicated, defenses needed to find a way to keep up.

Tampa Bay's Antoine Winfield Jr., *left*, and Jordan Whitehead celebrate after Winfield's interception during Super Bowl LV.

Steve Owen and his defensive coordinator, future Hall of Fame Dallas Cowboys coach Tom Landry, did that when they created the 4–3 defense in the 1950s. But offenses evolved. In 1960 the Philadelphia Eagles were preparing to face the Green Bay Packers in the NFL title game. Green Bay featured

Few cornerbacks were faster or more effective in man-to-man coverage than Hall of Famer Deion Sanders (21).

a potent offense. Eagles assistant coach Jerry Williams came up with something new to stop the Packers' passing game. He decided to take away a linebacker and add an additional defensive back to the defense. The plan worked. The Eagles beat the Packers 17–13.

That fifth defensive back became known as the nickel back. The formation became known as the nickel defense. The nickel allows teams to get more speed on the field when offenses line up three or more wide receivers. For years it was a special substitution package, used only when offenses had a long way to go for a first down and were more likely to pass. As teams started to pass more even on first down, nickel defenses became more common. In 2021 NFL defenses lined up in the nickel more than 61 percent of the time.

MAN VS. ZONE

Within formations designed to stop the pass, there are two ways defenses cover receivers—man-to-man (or simply man) and zone. In a man defense, a defender is assigned a specific player. He tracks that player's every move. The idea is to make the quarterback throw into tight coverage. That way a defender can try to knock down the pass or make an interception. However, it's easier for offenses to design quick passes to beat man coverage. That's especially true if the receiver has a speed advantage over his defender.

In zone coverage, every defender who isn't rushing the passer covers a specific area of the field. The goal in a zone is to make receivers work harder to get open. That way the quarterback has to hold on to the ball longer. If it works, pass rushers have a little more time to get into the backfield. However, every zone leaves some open spaces. If the pass rush can't get to the quarterback in time, he will likely find a receiver to target.

Both coverages have strengths and weaknesses, so a defense will usually mix up its calls to try to confuse the offense. There are also different kinds of ways to run both coverages. All of the schemes are based on how many players are covering the deep part of the field. In Cover 0, no one is playing deep. Teams blitz in Cover 0 to try to sack the quarterback or get him to rush a short throw that can be intercepted. Cover 1 and Cover 2 are common in both man and zone. Cover 1 has one safety deep. Cover 2 has both safeties deep. Cover 3 is the most common type of zone coverage in the NFL, with three players back deep. The rest cover the middle and both sides of the field.

In just one game a team may play every one of these coverages. What works best depends on what offense a defense is preparing for. Since the Buccaneers contained

Playing two safeties deep makes it hard for receivers to get open.

Patrick Mahomes in Super Bowl LV playing two deep safeties most of the game, the league has seen an increase in teams doing likewise. Defenses are trying to limit big passing plays, which have become more common. That was one reason scoring dropped in 2022. Average scoring per game per team was down almost three full points from 2020.

CHAPTER 5

NUMBERS GAME

Halftime was looming in Super Bowl LII in February 2018. The Philadelphia Eagles had worked the ball inside the New England Patriots' 2-yard line. With 38 seconds remaining, the Eagles were facing a fourth-and-goal situation. Philadelphia head coach Doug Pederson had a decision to make.

The Eagles were leading 15–12. Conventional football wisdom said to kick the short field goal for a six-point lead. If the Eagles went for it on fourth down and

Philadelphia Eagles quarterback Nick Foles was on the receiving end of a trick play during Super Bowl LII.

missed, Pederson knew he would be criticized for giving away three easy points.

Pederson took a timeout to think it over. He liked to take risks. And that didn't change on the game's biggest stage. The Eagles decided to go for it. During the timeout, Philadelphia quarterback Nick Foles suggested a play to run. Foles lined up in the shotgun formation. Then he wandered up toward the line of scrimmage and started yelling instructions to his linemen. It looked as if Foles was changing the play. As Foles moved toward the right tackle, center Jason Kelce snapped the ball to running back Corey Clement. Tight end Trey Burton ran to the right and took the ball from Clement. Meanwhile, Foles ran to the right side of the end zone. The quarterback was all alone when he caught a touchdown pass that put the Eagles up 22–12.

This trick play was called the "Philly Special." The play was a big risk. Running it on fourth down made it even riskier. But Pederson's decision to go for it was a sign of the times in the modern NFL.

A NEW WAY TO SCORE

Since 1958 college football teams that score a touchdown have had the option of kicking the extra point or going for a two-point conversion. Just as with an extra-point kick, the ball

Stephen Gostkowski made a record 523 consecutive extra-point kicks, a streak that ended in the 2015 playoffs after the line of scrimmage for such kicks was moved back to the 15-yard line.

was placed on the 2-yard line. A team could choose to run a play from there. If the team reached the end zone on that play, it scored two points. It made games more exciting, but the NFL didn't add the option for a two-point conversion until 1994.

The league adopted that rule to increase scoring and give teams a better chance to come back when they were trailing. Teams took to the new rule right away, attempting 113 two-point conversions in the 1994 season. They made

52 percent of them. But the excitement soon wore off. Teams steadily went for two less often and picked the safer option of kicking the extra point. In 2014 only 58 two-point conversions were attempted. That led the league to make another rule to encourage going for two. In 2015 the NFL moved the extra-point kick back from the 2-yard line to the 15. With the extra point now basically a 33-yard field goal, kickers started to miss them at a higher rate. Teams then did the math and figured out it was now more efficient to go for two.

This led to an increase in two-point attempts, but no team decided to go for two every time. Teams base their decision on the situation of the game. A decision that has become more popular is going for two when trailing by eight points late in the game. For example, a team scores a

While rare, defenses can score on a two-point conversion as well. This unlikely play helped the Kansas City Chiefs win a game in 2016. The Atlanta Falcons scored to go ahead 28–27 with 4:32 left in the game. A successful two-point conversion would ensure the Chiefs couldn't win on a field goal. However, Chiefs safety Eric Berry intercepted the Falcons' two-point conversion attempt. Then he ran it all the way back to the other end zone, giving Kansas City two points. The Chiefs won the game 29–28.

touchdown to cut its deficit to 24–16. Conventional wisdom says to kick the extra point to make it 24–17. Then another touchdown and extra point would tie the game.

However, it is mathematically more likely for a team to convert one two-point conversion than to fail twice. If the team scores and makes a two-point play, it will trail 24–18. Now a touchdown and extra-point kick would mean a 25–24 lead. If it misses on that two-point play, the team knows it must score

Tom Brady celebrates after picking up a key first down for his New England Patriots.

a touchdown and then convert a two-point play to tie. From 2000 to 2017, teams went for two in this scenario twice. But in the two-year span of 2018 and 2019, teams did this 12 times.

GO FOR IT

During a 2009 game, Patriots head coach Bill Belichick made a controversial decision. His team was leading 34–28 with 2:08 left against the Indianapolis Colts. But they faced fourth-and-two from their own 28-yard line. Belichick decided to go for it. If the Patriots made the first down, they would retain possession. They could then run out the clock and win the game. If the Patriots missed, they would put the Colts in prime position to score a game-winning touchdown.

The Colts stopped the Patriots. They then scored with 13 seconds left and won 35–34. Belichick was criticized for the decision at the time. But years later, this decision became more common in the NFL. Just as with two-point conversions, teams eventually realized the mathematical advantage of going for it on fourth down.

When Belichick made that decision, each NFL game featured an average of 1.09 fourth-down attempts per game. By 2021 that number was up to 1.46, the highest in NFL history. A big reason was the success rate. Teams were converting on fourth down 51 percent of the time. And the fewer yards they need to convert, the higher the chance they have of picking up the first down. From 2013 to 2022, NFL teams that ran plays on fourth-and-two were successful 57.2 percent of the time. That rose to 65.5 percent on fourth-and-one attempts. So while Belichick's decision in 2009 was unsuccessful, it was the correct call based on the numbers.

GLOSSARY

blitz
When a linebacker or defensive back attacks the line of scrimmage to stop a run or sack the quarterback.

controversial
Something that leads to a public dispute.

conventional wisdom
A generally accepted belief.

coordinator
An assistant coach who is in charge of the offense or defense.

line of scrimmage
The yard line on the field where a play starts.

motion
Movement by a player from his set spot before a play.

pocket
The area behind the line of scrimmage where the quarterback stands after dropping back to pass.

red zone
The area inside the 20-yard line at both ends of the field.

shotgun
A formation in which the quarterback lines up five to seven yards behind the center and takes the snap in the air.

versatility
Ability to perform many different roles or functions.

Books

Flynn, Brendan. *The NFL Encyclopedia*. Minneapolis, MN: Abdo Publishing, 2022.

Graves, Will. *GOATs of Football*. Minneapolis, MN: Abdo Publishing, 2022.

Hustad, Douglas. *Innovations in Football*. Minneapolis, MN: Abdo Publishing, 2022.

Online Resources

To learn more about football strategies, please visit **abdobooklinks.com** or scan this QR code. These links are routinely monitored and updated to provide the most current information available.

About the Author

Luke Hanlon is a sportswriter and editor based in Minneapolis.